By the same author

The Divided Self

Self and Others

Reason and Violence

Sanity, Madness and the Family
(with Aaron Esterson)

Interpersonal Perception

The Politics of Experience and The Bird of Paradise

Knots

The Politics of the Family

The Facts of Life

R. D. Laing

DO YOU LOVE ME?

An Entertainment in Conversation and Verse

Allen Lane

B

821
LA1

Allen Lane
Penguin Books Ltd,
17 Grosvenor Gardens, London SW1W 0BD

First published in the U.S.A. by Pantheon Books 1976
Published in Great Britain by Allen Lane 1977

ISBN 0 7139 0995 1

Set in 8 on 10 pt Rockwell

Printed in Great Britain by
Cox & Wyman Ltd, London, Fakenham and Reading

1   **Return of the Prodigal (I)**

mother	he's come back to see you
son	hullo dad
father	hello (*pause*) Who are you?
son	I'm your son dad
father	O you're my *son*
son	yes dad
father	and what's your name?
son	Peter
father	you're my son Peter
son	yes dad
father	you're my son Peter
son	yes dad I'm your son Peter
father	you used to live with my wife. I never thought I would see you again
son	well here I am dad
father	very nice to see you again Peter
son	very nice to see you again dad
father	and are you married Peter
son	yes dad
father	and have you any children
son	yes dad
father	and what have you been up to
son	I've been roaming around
father	and have you been successful
son	yes so far touch wood
father	that's wonderful that's wonderful and are you married Peter
son	yes dad
father	and have you any children
son	yes dad
father	and what do you do
son	I'm a musician
father	Peter was always interested in music
son	yes
father	are you staying long?
son	I have to leave in a few minutes
father	well I'm very glad to see you Peter
son	very glad to see you dad (*pause*)

1

son	how have *you* been keeping?
father	I don't want her to die before me
mother	you shouldn't say that
	(*pause*)
father	you're a musician
son	yes
father	my son Peter's a magician
	do you know him?
son	I'm not sure
father	he travels around a lot
	he's famous are you sure you don't know him?
son	I *am* him
father	O you *are* him
son	I'm your son Peter
father	you're my son Peter
	I never thought I would see you again Peter.
	That's wonderful do you hear that
	he's my son Peter
son	you got a son called Peter?
father	that's my boy
son	what do you think of Peter dad?
mother	that's enough!
son	why?
mother	you've already gone too far
son	be quiet it's alright
mother	you were always like that
son	don't interfere
mother	it's my business
son	what do you think of Peter?
father	(*laughing*) he's a bit of a rascal
mother	(*puts palm across father's mouth with outstretched arm and keeps it there, addressing son*)
	there will be no more of this nonsense
son	(*removes mother's hand from father's mouth with slow steady application of force – she resists silently with all her power, till her two hands are placed across her lap*)
	it's alright (*kisses her*) I promise
	I have to go now anyway

2

	(turns to father)
	I'm Peter I have to go now dad
father	well I'm very glad to see you Peter
	I never thought I would see you again
son	goodbye dad
	very glad to see you again
father	goodbye Peter. Wonderful
son	goodbye mum
	(kisses)
mother	don't be so long next time
son	I won't
	(kisses)

I couldn't believe it I just couldn't believe it just could not
believe it I I I just couldn't believe it couldn't believe it
couldn't believe it I just couldn't believe it couldn't believe it
couldn't believe it I I just I just couldn't I just couldn't
believe it could not believe it I couldn't believe it couldn't
believe it couldn't believe it

do y'know what I mean you know y'know what I mean it's sort
of it's well it's it's well it's you know what I mean y'know you
just can't have any idea y'know what I mean y'know it's it's
well it's not like anything really you know what I mean it's
nothing really d'you know what I mean I can't stand it

What am I going on about anyway? whats the problem? is
there a problem? thats the problem. maybe. maybe not. but
anyway. why do I think there may be a problem if there is
no problem and why do I think there may be no problem if
there is? anyway. whether there is or there isnt a problem
its a problem how much time to spend figuring out if there
is or there isn't anyway what difference does it make anyway
if there is or is not a problem what *is* a problem is a problem
anyway

no thinking no no thinking no no no *no* thinking
no no no no no no thinking no forgetting no recall
no action no no action *do* nothing don't
do nothing don't do anything what is not allowed is forbidden

My neck is on the guillotine the blade comes down
my head goes this way the rest goes that
which side will I be on?

3

Little old shop, evening, December
Young Man, overcoat, bottle of red wine in hand,
enters from front door.
Old Man enters from back of shop to behind
counter.

old man	Good morning
young man	(*pauses, then, abruptly*) Good morning . . .
old man	Yes?
young man	Yes. Sorry. Have you a corkscrew please?
old man	Why?
young man	(*pauses, then abruptly*)
	I want to open this bottle
old man	(*quickly, and as though that explains it*)
	Oh I see
	(*pause*)
young man	Well?
old man	(*pleasantly and patiently*) What?
young man	Have you a corkscrew?
old man	No
young man	Well tha—
old man	(*interrupts*) I'm sorry. I haven't.
young man	Well th—
old man	(*interrupts*) No I'm very sorry I haven't
	(*pause*)
	Have you tried elsewhere?
young man	Yes. I have
old man	Did they have one?
young man	No they didn't
old man	Did you try up the road?
young man	Yes I did
old man	Did they have one?
young man	No they did not
old man	It's no use trying up the road,
	they never have anything
young man	Well then
old man	(*interrupts*) Have you tried *down* the road?
young man	No. I have not
old man	(*with sudden finality*) Try down the road!

5

young man	Yes well thanks. I shall. Yes thank you very much
old man	Not at all my pleasure goodday
young man	Goodday

4

I've lost it
lost what?
have you seen it?
seen what?
my face
no

5

doctor   How are you?
*The patient points to a tracheotomy tube in his
neck*
doctor   I'm sorry
*Realizing the patient can't speak,
the doctor takes a pad and pencil and writes*

How are you?

*and hands pad and pencil to the patient for his
reply
The patient takes the pad and pencil and writes*

I'm not deaf

6

Red spiders did you say?
>with green eyes

When did it start?
>when I left her

Still going on?
>they stopped some months ago
>now it's vampires seven feet across with green
>eyes close together one nearly got me the other
>day

How?
>I was off guard I was in the bath just relaxing
>into some nice Nepalese one of them came at me

What happened?
>it had breached my psychic defence shield. It got
>to a foot of my throat

And?
>I stopped it by mind control but it was close

You can't be too careful
>too true

When are you seeing her again?
>tomorrow

Best of luck

7

You're jewish aren't you?
               yes
You don't look jewish, you know what I mean
               no
You're not *orthodox*, are you, or anything like that?
               O no
There's no anti-semitism here, you know, so you shouldn't
have any problems, you know what I mean
               good good
No you shouldn't have any problems (*pause*)
You're sure you're not orthodox?
               O no I'm a psychoanalyst
O yes of course no you shouldn't have
any problems just say you're presbyterian you know
what I mean

Return of the Prodigal (II)

Father!

Bastard!

Father!

Bastard!

Barnacle Bill's my father

I'm Barnacle Bill

Father!

Bastard!

9

Jack and Jill are married and love each other
Jack from time to time thinks Jill has affairs
with Tom, Dick or Harry, but he is wrong

Jack's best friend is John
John's wife leaves him, and Jack invites John
to stay with him and Jill

While Jill is consoling John, John fucks Jill:
Jill thus discovers that Jack can't trust John

Enraged at John's betrayal of Jack,
she tells Jack he can't trust John, but not why
Jack feels Jill is jealous of John and him and is trying
to break up their friendship

Jack leaves Jill

Jack and John go off together

10

Jack and Jill are married, in love, and have children

Jack thinks Jill is having an affair with Tom
his best friend
He confides in Jane, Jill's best friend,
who confirms his suspicions

So does Tom

Jill denies everything
Jack can no longer believe her
He leaves Jill and the children
and goes to live with Jane

Jill goes to live with Tom

Actually, it was Jane and Tom who were the secret lovers:
a fact Jack and Jill never knew

11

Jack, Dick and Tom are best friends
Jill, Jane and Joan are best friends

Jack and Jill fall in love
Dick and Jane fall in love

Jack and Joan fall in love
Tom falls in love with Joan
Joan falls out of love with Jack and into love with Tom
Jane falls in love with Tom
Tom falls out of love with Joan and into love with Jane
Jack falls out of love with Joan and into love with Jane

Jane has Jack, Dick and Tom

Joan kills herself

Jane falls out of love with Tom
and into love with Dick again

Jack falls out of love with Jane
and into love with Jill again

Dick and Jill do not know about
Jack and Jane, Jack and Joan, Tom and Jane, Tom and Joan

Tom does not know about Jack and Jane

13

(*he puts on some music*)
(*after a little*)

she   how about some music
(*he takes record off, and puts on another*)
(*she takes that one off and puts on another*)
(*after a little*)

she   do you like it?

he   not particularly
(*pause*) but I don't mind it (*pause*)
no one's dancing
(*she puts on another*)

he   couldn't you put on something a bit
more personal?
(*she takes it off and puts on another without
comment*)
(*they sit in silence till the end of side 1*)

she   I don't know what to put on now?

he   don't put on anything then

she   but I would like *something*

he   then put on something you know and like

she   do you know this one?

he   no. Do you?

she   no
(*she puts it on*)
(*after a bit*)

he   why can't you put on something we both
know and like or *you* at least know and
like. I don't like our home being invaded
by a crowd of complete strangers

she   I quite like it

he   I don't
(*she takes it off. Puts on the first one
she had on before*)

she   I know and like this
(*he takes it off. Puts on another*)

he   I *love* this one
(*he turns the volume up*)

she   would you mind turning it down a bit, please?
(*he turns it down*)

14

she	can I change it? No I'll wait
he	I think I'm entitled to one side
	(*she turns it down a bit more*)
he	I can't hear it now (*pause*). Mind if I turn
	it up a little?
she	no
	(*he turns it up a little*)
she	you never look at me
he	I beg your pardon
she	I'm not going to shout
	(*he turns it down*)
she	you never look at me
	(*he turns it up again*)

13

he	what do you want?
she	make love to me
he	you are a
	placenta that sucks me dry and poisons me
	a womb that suffocates and crushes me
	an umbilical cord that stings and strangles me
	your vagina is the entry to hell
	not tonight Josephine
she	you would put anyone off
he	put out the light
she	you have put it out yourself

14

he	how about it?
she	not like that
he	I fancy you more than you fancy me
she	that's because you are emotionally blocked
he	how do you make that out?
she	you can't stand your feelings,
	so you put them all into your penis
he	you have less time for me
	than I have for you
she	you mean you want to fuck me more often
	than I want to be fucked
he	I like looking into your eyes
she	emotionally mature people do not seem
	to need to look into one another's eyes
	as long and as often as you seem to need
	to look into mine
he	your face is beautiful in the firelight
she	no doubt I remind you of your mother
he	mummy!
she	not tonight Oedipus

16

15

she	you were going to ask me what I wanted for a birthday present
he	O yes. I forgot. What would you like?
she	guess
he	the head of John the Baptist
she	don't be frivolous
he	what then?
she	a divorce
he	it's too expensive
she	O darling please
he	I'll see what I can do but I can't promise
she	promise you'll do your best
he	promise
she	(*kisses*)
he	(*kisses*)

16

he	I can't hear you
she	you're not listening
he	I'm trying
she	I love you for *trying*
he	I was trying to acknowledge I heard you
she	I detest being acknowledged
he	alright
she	it's not alright
he	what's not?
she	you're not listening
he	you're not communicating
she	the dumb speak to the deaf
he	there we are
she	don't do that
he	am I not allowed to agree with you
she	it's not funny
he	I never said it was

17

he	it's difficult
she	difficult
he	difficult to stop
she	very difficult
he	especially
she	yes
he	when
she	quite
he	it's difficult
she	let's stop it
	(*pause*)
he	stopped
she	stopped
	(*pause*)
	(*almost simultaneously*)
she	Oh
he	it's started again
she	let's stop it
he	how?
she	stopped
	(*pause*)
she	(*talking about it*)
	it is difficult
he	what *is* it?
	(*pause*)
she	it's started again
he	stopped
	(*pause*)
she ⎫ he ⎭	you're at it again you're at it again
	(*pause*)
she ⎫ he ⎭	difficult it is difficult

18

she	stop it
he	you stop it
she	I can't stop what I'm not doing
he	you started it
she	and you stop it
he	I can't stop what I'm not doing
she	you think you're going to get away with it
he	get away with what?
she	you're not going to wriggle out of it this time
he	wriggle out of what
she	don't kid you're daft
he	I'm not doing anything of the kind
she	come off it
he	I'm not on it
she	cut it out
he	cut what out?
she	will you stop it
he	stop what?
she	that
he	what?
she	you know perfectly well
he	I'm afraid I don't
she	I'm afraid I don't
he	I'm going to sleep
she	you've never woken up

19

she	where does it all come from?
he	all what come from?
she	all that shit you keep pouring over me all the time
he	count your blessings
she	I'm counting my toes
he	the Lord giveth the Lord taketh away
she	you should have told me
he	what?
she	that I was living with the Lord God Almighty
he	what's the matter now?
she	you obviously think you're the Lord God Almighty
he	can't you moderate your language
she	Lord Muck that's what you are Lord Muck
he	I am not the Lord God Almighty and I am not Lord Muck
she	really?
he	yes really
she	you're such a liar

20

she	you think you're going to get away with it
he	get away with what?
she	you hate women, you destroy women.
	Look at all the women you've destroyed
he	look at them
she	take a good look at them
he	I've no particular desire to
she	well?
he	well what?
she	you're not going to do that to me
he	do what to you?
she	what you've done to them
he	what have I done to them?
she	look at them
he	well
she	you've cut them up and stuffed the pieces
	and you have them here plastered all around us.
	You're not going to cut me up and stuff me like
	that
he	really, I can't see anything
she	I can *smell* it
he	your nose is too near your arse

she	well then
he	well then what?
she	you know
he	I know what?
she	you know perfectly well
he	No I do not know perfectly well
she	come on
he	you come on
she	come off it
he	you come off it
she	you give it up
he	you started it
she	it's you that's keeping it going
he	what going?
she	you're still at it
he	at what?
she	you know perfectly well
he	I'm not going into that again
she	you've never gone into anything
he	look who's talking
she	I'm looking

she	well then?
he	well then what?
she	you did didn't you?
he	what are you talking about?
she	you know perfectly well what I'm talking about
he	if you're still on about that I've said all I am going to say
she	you did didn't you?
he	I've already told you
she	you did didn't you?
he	I'm not going to be interrogated
she	just tell me the truth
he	I've told you
she	who was it?
he	no one
she	you're such a liar
he	you said you weren't jealous
she	don't change the subject
he	what are you going on about? I've already told you
she	I'm not jealous I only have to know
he	why have you such a suspicious mind?
she	I know who it was
he	you've made up your mind. There's nothing more I can say
she	you think you're going to get away with it
he	there's nothing to get away with
she	you did I know you did
	(*pause*)
he	no
she	you might as well admit it
he	there's nothing to admit
she	she told me herself
he	I know you are making that up
she	she came and told me herself
he	why do you have to resort to such lies?
she	I'm not going to let you destroy my sense of reality along with everything else
he	you are paranoid

she	you're not going to get away with it
he	you fancy her yourself
she	no
he	you're an unconscious lesbian
she	no
he	you should see a psychiatrist
she	don't fob me off
he	you're obsessed
she	you did I know you did
	(*pause*)
	I'll phone her up right now
	(*pause*)
	you did
	(*pause*)
he	once
she	you're such a liar
he	I didn't enjoy it
she	O you're such a fuckin liar

23

he	darling please forgive me
she	I've forgiven you for everything already
he	please forgive me one more time
she	there's nothing more to forgive
he	don't despair darling
she	no?
he	darling please forgive me
she	I've forgiven you so much I'm exhausted please
he	but darling I can't come if you don't forgive me
she	try going then
he	but darling if you don't forgive me I *have* to again so you'll forgive me again
she	I'll never forgive you
he	you're so arrogant
she	I'll never forgive you for anything any more
he	but you can't *help* it darling
she	no?
he	you can't keep it up don't worry it'll be alright
she	I mean it
he	I'll give you something else to forgive
she	not for my sake please
he	not at all, I like helping along your spiritual development

24

she	it's the same thing
he	no it is not
she	yes it is
he	let's not go through all that again
she	right
he	why do you always have the last word?
she	you have it
he	thank you
	(*pause*)
she	don't mention it
he	why can't you shut up
she	why can't *you* shut up
he	shut up
she	you shut up
	(*both together*)
he ⎫	shut up
she ⎭	shut up

she	I can't help it
he	can't help what?
she	getting into this
he	getting into what?
she	if I could say I wouldn't be in it
he	what's it like?
she	it's terrible
he	in what way?
she	I can't say. That's why it's so terrible
he	try harder
she	I'm doing my best
he	your best is not good enough however
she	I know
he	you're very blasé about it
she	I'm desperate
he	where were we?
she	I don't know
he	what do you mean you don't know?
she	what do you mean what do I mean?
he	what were you saying?
she	I was saying I can't help it
he	can't help what?
she	getting into this
he	this what?
she	what we are in now
he	what are you talking about?
she	(*silence*)
he	you must have been talking about something
she	I can't say
he	what do you mean you can't say?
she	I can't say
he	why don't you stop it?
she	you know perfectly well
he	I do not
she	don't you?
he	no
she	why don't I stop what?
he	being less difficult
she	I'm doing my best to be cooperative

he	your best is not good enough however
she	I'm trying
he	answer my question then.
she	what question?
he	why are you so negative?
she	I'm not negative
he	that's what you're like
she	that's not what I'm like
he	that's how you are
she	no that's not how I am
he	yes it is
she	no it's not
he	you can't help it?
she	I can't help it
he	yes you can
she	no I can't
he	and you're not negative?
she	no
he	what are you then?
she	I don't know any more
he	you can't help being what you are
she	I'm not what I am
he	yes you are
she	no I am not
he	what are you then?
she	(*silence*)
he	there you are then
she	(*silence*)
he	you're yourself
she	I'm not myself
he	why are you so negative?
she	I'm not negative
he	stop playing games with me
she	I can't help it
he	just give it up
she	give what up?
he	your defences
she	and then what?
he	what's your fantasy?

28

she	I don't know who I am
he	why can't you be less self-centred?
she	I've no identity except the one you give me
he	you think about yourself too much
she	I haven't got a self
he	you're self-contradictory
she	I can't help it
he	why don't you let me help you?
she	how?
he	by being more cooperative
she	how?
he	answer my question
she	what was your question?
he	I'm asking the questions not answering them for the moment
she	what was your question then?
he	why are you so difficult?
she	I'm not difficult
he	what were you complaining about then?
she	I wasn't complaining
he	why do you contradict me all the time?
she	I don't contradict you all the time
he	what were you doing just now?
she	I disagreed with you
he	you feel you must compete with me
she	I'm not trying to compete with you
he	it's not a question of winning
she	I never said it was
he	and you call that not being difficult?
she	yes
he	and you're not playing games?
she	no
he	what are you going on about then?
she	I wasn't going on about anything
he	you must have been going on about something
she	I just wish I could get out of this
he	what are you really complaining about?
she	I'm not complaining
he	have you a bad memory?

29

she	no
he	can't you see I'm trying to help you?
she	yes I can see you're trying to help me
he	why don't you let me help you then?
she	I never asked you to help me
he	can't you see you can't get out of this yourself?
she	that's what I'm saying
he	why won't you let me help you then?
she	your help is like salt water to a drowning man
he	there you are
she	no I'm not
he	why are you like you are?
she	I'm not like I am
he	what are you like then?
she	nothing
he	you're impossible
she	I can't help it
he	can't help what?
she	getting into this
he	what are you complaining about?
she	I'm not complaining
he	you have a bad memory?
she	no
he	why can't you remember then?
she	remember what?
he	how long you've had it?
she	had what?
he	your complaint
she	I am not complaining
he	what are you doing then?
she	I was saying I can't help it
he	I believe you can
she	I can't
he	it's the word of hope
she	it's hopeless
he	do not despair
she	I can't help it
he	can't help what?
she	getting into this

30

he	getting into what?
she	into this
he	and what is this?
she	this (*pause*) this
he	you are not making any sense
she	I know
he	why do you go on like this then?
she	I wish I could stop
he	why don't you stop then?
she	I can't help it
he	you wouldn't go on like this if you were yourself
she	I wish we could stop getting into this
he	into what?
she	into this
he	and what is this?
she	this (*pause*) this
he	try to be more explicit
she	I'm being as explicit as I can
he	what are you going on about?
she	I'm not going on about anything
he	what are you up to?
she	I'm not up to anything
he	what are you saying then?
she	I've said it before
he	say it again
she	I've said it for the umpteenth time
he	what is it?
she	I wish I could out of here
he	out of what?
she	what we're in now
he	what's that?
she	it's endless
he	can't you see I'm trying to help you?
she	O my god
he	what's the matter?
she	you
he	there you go again
she	leave me alone
he	I'm not molesting you

31

she	Oh yes yes yes you are
he	you know you know that's not true
she	I don't think I'm going to be able to control myself much longer
he	what do you suppose you will do?
she	when?
he	when you give it up
she	what up?
he	this up
she	and what is this?
he	what you're doing
she	I wish I wasn't here
he	you feel suicidal?
she	I don't seem to be able to help it
he	you are denying your responsibility
she	I can't tell you anything
he	try to be less global
she	that's what I mean
he	for instance
she	it's like talking to a wall or any empty space
he	you cannot even admit my existence as another human person like yourself
she	there's no one there
he	I feel that
she	feel what?
he	you're not there
she	what's the use?
he	you're depressed
she	I'm desperate
he	because you can't allow me to help you
she	how?
he	you need my help to help you realize you need it
she	please stop trying to help me
he	I can't help it
she	can't help what?
he	there's nothing much to be done I'm afraid
she	done about what?
he	you

32

she	I didn't ask you to do anything about me
he	what were you asking then?
she	I wasn't asking anything
he	why are you here then?
she	I was saying I couldn't help always coming back to the same place
he	what are you complaining about?
she	I'm just saying that each moment with you is better than the next
he	you are pushing your feelings away now
she	I don't feel that
he	I'm sorry, I forgot, you can't help it
she	this is awful
he	you can't feel anything?
she	please don't try to make me feel something
he	I know you don't really mean that
she	really I don't want to feel anything
he	are you a robot?
she	please (*stretches out hand*) I'm not a robot
he	I'm not wasting my precious time on a filthy robot
she	I'm not a robot
he	stop acting like one then
she	I can't help it
he	maybe you can't
she	I wouldn't be here if I could help it
he	I'm trying to help
she	don't take offence
he	don't flatter yourself
she	I tried not to
he	not to what?
she	not to offend you
he	you haven't offended me
she	I feel I have
he	you are at the stage of infantile omnipotence
she	have I offended you?
he	you tell me it's your fantasy
she	I can't say
he	what can't you say?
she	if I have offended you

33

he	you feel you have offended me?
she	yes
he	you felt you offended me just now?
she	I'm not sure
he	perhaps it was your imagination?
she	perhaps
he	perhaps it wasn't
she	it wasn't my imagination?
he	you're at it again
she	how?
he	you're at it now
she	what?
he	you know perfectly well
she	no I do not
he	here and now
she	I don't know what you are talking about
he	will you stop it?
she	stop what?
he	what you're doing this very instant
she	living
he	do you call what you're doing living?
she	I'm doing my best
he	your best is not good enough however
she	I can't help it
he	can't help what?

26   take this pill
to help you not to shout.
It takes away the life
you're better off without.

27   the trouble with you
's you've lost a screw

I'm sorry it's you
but there's nothing to do

there'll be no abatements
there are no replacements

don't make a to-do
just say toodle-oo

I'm sorry I can't help you
you'd cost too much to redo

you'll have to be abolished
report to be demolished

28   is he trying to amuse me
to confound and confuse me?
does he bring me home flowers
in order to use me?

I tell her I love her
because I hate her
I'm nice to her now
to do her in later.

does he kiss me and pet me
just to perplex me?
if I cut my throat
will he aid and abet me?

after she's gone
I'll quickly forget her
go on the prowl
and find something better.

29   she's nasty to me
so I'm nasty to her

she follows me
so I follow her

30   they say that good intentions
pave the road to hell
if a thing is not worth doing
it's not worth doing well

31   I dreamt I was a butterfly
dreaming it was me
it looked into a mirror
there was nothing there to see

'you lie'
        I cried
it woke
        I died

32   sometimes I come
sometimes I go
but which is which
I don't know

sometimes I am
sometimes I'm not
but which is which
I forgot

33   I dreamt I was a dead rat
in a city sewer
I started to rust
and turned to dust
until I was no more

34

Why is there she?
Why is there me?
Why why why?   Why why why?   Why why why?

I can't even see
why a flea
is so wee
let alone
where I'll be
when I die

Why is there she?
Why is there he?
Why why why?   Why why why?   Why why why?

I can't even see
where it goes
when I pee
let alone
where I'll be
when I die

35   mummy'll scream
if you have a wet dream

do not let frustration
lead to masturbation

little Billy
plays with his willy
that's why he's silly

36   where's the pleasure?
where's the fun?

is this only
one long bum run?

is what seemed joy
one more decoy?

where's the delight
I took in your sight?

is there a morning
to follow this night?

37   hello (*casually*)
yes it is (*absently*)
no (*uncuriously*)
really (*with some surprise*)
whose was it (*out of politeness*)?
mine (*incredulously*)!
when (*challengingly*)?
really (*interestedly*)
ah ha (*reminiscently*)
mmmm (*musingly*)
you should have told me (*ironically*)
a pity I couldn't have had it for you (*gleefully*)
there it is (*grimly*)
give me a ring sometime (*dutifully*)
you could always have another (*brutally*)
c'est la vie (*consolingly*)
goodbye (*sincerely*)

38   the die is cast
you're breathing your last
no more will you roam

your breath has a smell
that's straight from hell
you've found your Home Sweet Home

40

39   you can rant and rave
I won't be your slave
or another gap to fill in

it's none too soon
for a new spittoon
and something else to shit in

40   why do you lie in bed
soft in the head
on a cold and frosty morning?

the other side of light
isn't very bright
I didn't heed the gypsy's warning

41   do I hurt you
when I touch you?

was that a shiver
or a quiver?

tell me where
you're there

taunt me
haunt me
as long as you want me

42

you'll cry
when I die

you'll yawn
when I'm gone

you'll be bored
unadored

43

cross your fingers
tell me your woes
there are lies that linger
cross your nose
if Cain were able
he would give you a rose

44

was that a kiss?

or a hiss

from the abyss?

45   I liked to eat mice
that was then
I was ten
now it's men
they're not as nice

46   I could tell
            from your eyes
you fell
            from the skies

        out of the blue
        there were you

but I knew it wasn't true
and away
    you flew

47   Daisy, Daisy,
what are we going to do?
I'm half crazy
I'm in love and in hate with you

    although I'm so contrary
    at least I'm not a fairy

    'twould break my heart
    if we should part
    it's already divided in two

You're gonna get it
you're gonna live to regret it
        if only you'll marry me
        if only you'll marry me

You won't forget me in a hurry
I'll make you sorry, make you worry
        if only you'll marry me
        if only you'll marry me

I'll squash you like a fly
make you squish and squirm and fry
        if only you'll marry me
        if only you'll marry me

I'll mate you and bait you
and settle down to hate you
        if only you'll marry me
        if only you'll marry me

We'll live a life of misery
        if only you'll marry me

49

you were a nice little gay thing
a bird that only could sing
but joy began to cloy
for you were not a boy
some bell just wouldn't ring

you were a pretty safe plaything
a bee without a sting

I took my chances
with other romances

we had a fight
I proved I was right

you were second best
but now you've left

I'm a yoyo without a string

The Song of the False Guru's Wife

If only it were as easy
as they try to make it sound
I'd always be chirpy and cheery
and whirl round and round and round
and whirl round and round and round

but

his Chakras are filled up with sawdust
his Kundalini is coiled up in glue
his third eye is stuffed with broken glass
and I don't know what to do

When I'm washing the dishes
when I take out the children to play
I often feel I'd rather be dead
if things go on this way
if things go on this way

for

his Chakras are filled up with sawdust
his Kundalini is coiled up in glue
his third eye is stuffed with broken glass
and I don't know what to do

When I open my eyes in the morning
when I shut them tight at night
there he's sneering and jeering and leering
and from him comes a foul white light
and from him comes a foul white light

for

his Chakras are filled up with sawdust
his Kundalini is coiled up in glue
his third eye is stuffed with broken glass
and I don't know what to do

His veins are clogged with mercury
I'm certain it's not right
the bells of hell shall ring his knell
for in his heart is night
for in his heart is night

for

his Chakras are filled up with sawdust
his Kundalini is coiled up in glue
his third eye is stuffed with broken glass
and I don't know what to do

51

I swooned for the moon
            but didn't get it

I peed in the sea
            but didn't wet it

I poked the sun with a pole
            but only made a hole

but

though I may be dim
if the sea tries to swim
            I'll net it

I swallowed the stars
            but still was hollow

I turned back the years
            there's still tomorrow

I've offered God a role
but He's out of my control

I'm a pig in a poke
an awfully bad joke
            I can't follow

I was discontented
with girls that were rented
so I had invented my own

I could switch her on
I could switch her off

she used to make me feel
I was quite a toff
    but now it's my night to moan

she was mainly plastic
her arteries were elastic
and her voice was electronic monotone

she had a lovely hole
that was easy to control

I tried not to fondle her
in case I'd grow fond of her
    but now it's my night to moan

I was her maker
and I could break her
if she didn't answer the telephone

one day I broke her heart
but I'd lost the spare part

that's when she packed up
and then I cracked up
    so now it's my turn to moan to moan

53

As I was going along a road
I met a man, a bull a god

He whisked me off to heaven
To be his concubine:
But madam didn't like it
So now I'm worse than swine.

He promised me the earth
Gave me a present of the sky
He offered me a moonbeam
To wear if I was shy.

He said I was a treasure
Money couldn't buy.
He knew just how to make me laugh
Just when he'd made me cry.

He taught me not to worry
To forget it when he came.
He thought it would be better
If I didn't give the baby his name.

54

In days of old
when knights were bold
and women were just being invented

they locked up their wives
and fled for their lives
but never were contented

now times have changed
and those knights of yore
have no more armoured plating

it's wipe your bum
before you come
and no more masturbating

Still happy days will come again
we're meant for more than mating

but now we must
bite the dust

can't keep the ladies waiting

yes
happy days will come again
of that you can be sure

when women were women
and men were men
and we had pure manure

55

I went down to St James's infirmary
to see my love dying there
I went down to St James's infirmary
my own true love was dying there

It was first thing in the morning
both the moon and the sun were there
it was first thing in the morning
she left me gazing at her dead stare

It was down at St James's infirmary
who knows if it's fair
they wouldn't let me kiss her
they said she wasn't there

They took her own sweet body
they stuffed her own sweet nose
they tied her toes together
they wouldn't let me have her clothes

Maybe I don't see it
but they didn't seem to care
that my own true love had left me
standing helpless there

56

refugees from the sixth dimension
take care when you mention
what's past recollection

the womb
's a tomb
death
's our first breath

out of the furnace
into the mire
out of the frying pan
into the fire

you may regret,
or, better, forget it
or tell a faded story
sans glory

but if you confess it
if you try to tell them
what they do not want to know

they'll pickle you in piddle
frizzle you in drizzle
fry you in the snow

because they're wetter
doesn't mean you're better

to be emphatic
to be is not to be dogmatic

to be sceptic
to be is not to be erratic

one man's jubilation
's another's lamentation

your hallucination
's beyond their station

57
now
if not for ever
is
sometimes
better than never

58
is there a unicorn in your eyes?
tell no lies

did the swordfish
pierce the moon?

answer soon

59

when I try
from Zen sickness to fly

I'm sometimes low
and I'm sometimes high

sometimes I'm in
sometimes I'm out

sometimes I sing
and sometimes I **Shout**

sometimes I just laze around
sometimes I go underground

but

nevertheless
I must confess
it all seems less
than second best

without the one for whom I care
to pick my nose
and pull my hair

60

love is like the falling snow
once it comes it has to go

never say so, it's a lie
love's for ever, 'tis time must fly

61

I die forlorn
I was not born

I deny
I'm a butterfly

I'm a blot
I am not

I'm a fight no one fought
I'm a cold no one caught

I'm the Self-Appointed
Lord's Anointed

I'm a turd
I'm absurd

I'm a twinkling light
in some one else's night

I'm an insoluble riddle
I'm a hole with no middle

I'm going to hell
to yell
and smell

I fiddle
when I piddle

I'm a nitwit
I'm a titbit

I'm a kinkie
like a pinkie

I'm a flower with no name
I grow all the same

I'm a piece of fluff
in the huff

Never learned the game
I left before I came

mean
to
scream

I'm a dot
God forgot

I'm past mending
I'm a happy ending

she	Do you love me?
he	Yes I love you
she	Best of all?
he	Yes best of all
she	More than the whole world?
he	Yes more than the whole world
she	Do you like me?
he	Yes I like you
she	Do you like being near me?
he	Yes I like being near you
she	Do you like to look at me?
he	Yes I like looking at you
she	Do you think I'm stupid?
he	No I don't think you're stupid
she	Do you think I'm attractive?
he	Yes I think you're attractive
she	Do I bore you?
he	No you don't bore me
she	Do you like my eyebrows?
he	Yes I like your eyebrows
she	Very much?
he	Very much
she	Which one do you like the most?
he	If I say one the other will be jealous
she	You have to say
he	They are both exquisite
she	Honest?
he	Honest
she	Have I got nice eyelashes?
he	Yes nice nice eyelashes
she	Is that all?
he	They are exquisite
she	Do you like to smell me?
he	Yes I like to smell you
she	Do you like my perfume?
he	Yes I like your perfume
she	Do you think I've good taste?
he	Yes I think you have good taste
she	Do you think I'm talented?

he	Yes I think you're talented
she	You don't think I'm lazy?
he	No I don't think you're lazy
she	Do you like to touch me?
he	Yes I like to touch you
she	Do you think I'm funny?
he	Only in a nice way
she	Are you laughing at me?
he	No I'm not laughing at you
she	Do you really love me?
he	Yes I really love you
she	Say 'I love you'
he	I love you
she	Do you want to hug me?
he	Yes I want to hug you, and cuddle you, and bill and coo with you
she	Is it alright?
he	Yes it's alright
she	Swear you'll never leave me?
he	I swear I'll never ever leave you, cross my heart and hope to die if I tell a lie (*silence*)
she	Do you *really* love me?